Moments for Graduates

by Robert Strand

First printing, February 1994
Sixth printing, January 2006

ISBN: 0-89221-264-0
Library of Congress Catalog Number: 93-87691

Cover design by Left Coast Design, Portland, OR

All Scripture references are from the New International Version, unless otherwise noted.

New Leaf Press
A Division of New Leaf Publishing Group
www.newleafpress.net

Printed in China

Presented to:

_____

Presented by:

_____

Date:

_____

What Is Success?

In 1923, a group of the world's most successful financiers met at a Chicago hotel. Among those present were the president of the largest independent steel company in the world, the president of the largest utility company, the most successful commodity speculator, the president of the New York Stock Exchange, the president of the Bank of International Settlements, and the head of the world's greatest monopoly at that time.

Together these tycoons of the business world controlled more wealth than the treasury of the United States (remember that we were on the gold standard at that time). For years the media had been printing and talking about the success stories of these wealthy men. They had been held up as examples for all to follow, especially the youth of our nation. These men were at the very pinnacle of success in their world.

Let's take another look and see what happened to these men twenty-five years later.

Charles Schwab was the president of the largest independent steel company in the world. Twenty-five years later, he was living on borrowed money for the last five years of his life and died penniless. Incidentally, he was the first man in American history to draw an annual salary of $1 million.

Arthur Cutten, the greatest and most successful of commodity speculators, died abroad in dire poverty.

Richard Whitney, the president of the New York Stock Exchange, was sentenced to serve a term in Sing Sing Prison.

Albert Fall, who was a member of the president's Cabinet, was pardoned from prison so he could die at home.

Leon Fraser, president of the Bank of International Settlement, ended his life by committing suicide.

Ivar Kreuger, the head of the world's then greatest monopoly, put an end to the misery of his life by committing suicide.

All of these men, considered at one time the very epitome of success, had learned how to make money — and lots of it. I'm sure they saved, studied, worked long hours, disciplined themselves, and set their goals to reach the top of their chosen fields. But in the final analysis, not one of them had really learned how to live. Life is much more than accumulating riches or material things.

Jesus still has the right perspective on life.

Today's Quote: *Some men think they have made a success of life when all they have made is money!* — Author unknown

Today's Verse: "Beware! Don't always be wishing for what you don't have. For real life and real living are not related to how rich we are" (Luke 12:15;LB).

A Goal for Life

One of the most fascinating stories of goal setting comes out of the sports world. An eight-year-old boy told everyone who would listen, "I am going to be the greatest baseball catcher that ever lived!"

People would laugh at him and say, "Dream, you silly boy."

His mother patiently told him, "You are only eight years old, that's not the time to be talking about impossible dreams." He refused to listen to those who would attempt to talk him out of his goal.

When he finished his high school career and walked across the platform to get his diploma, the superintendent of schools stopped him and said, "Johnny, tell these people what you want to be."

The young man smiled, squared his shoulders, and said, "I am going to be the greatest baseball catcher that ever lived!" And you could hear the snickers across that graduation crowd.

The rest is history. On one occasion, the former great manager of the New York Yankees, Casey Stengel, was asked about this young man. Casey replied to the question like this: "Johnny Bench is already the greatest baseball catcher that ever played the game!"

What makes this story so amazing? Already, at age eight, Johnny Bench had set his goal in life. During his playing career, he was twice voted the most outstanding player in baseball. It began as a dream, then became a goal that was translated into reality.

Statistics tell me that if I were to poll each of you, less than 5 percent could say what their life goal is! Ninety-five out of every one hundred people are simply floating along on the tides of life.

Where are you planning to go with your life? Setting a goal for your life may well be the most important thing you will ever do! The starting point in any achievement begins with a goal! The apostle Paul knew the power of a life-goal when he said, "This one thing I do . . . ."

People with goals push ahead in the roughest, toughest, and most impossible kinds of situations and accomplish what they have set out to do.

Many of life's greatest achievements have yet to be met! Will you be one of those who sets a goal and discovers that your life can be changed and productive for the good of mankind? What is stopping you?

Today's Quote: *The Lord gave you two ends . . . one for sitting and one for thinking. Your success depends on which you use . . . Heads you win, tails you lose!* — Gas Flame

Today's Verse: . . . this one thing I do, forgetting those things which are behind, and reaching forth unto those things which are before, I press toward the mark for the prize of the high calling of God in Christ Jesus (Phil. 3:13–14;KJV).

Experience Counts

Hank, a landscape contractor, had landed his first, full-fledged job. Of course he didn't want to appear to be the rank amateur he knew he was, so he pretended a casual kind of nonchalance and expertise.

One of the first tasks he had to tackle was blasting out a farmer's tree stumps with dynamite. Since the farmer was watching, Hank went to some length to measure out the fuse and set the dynamite. So far so good, and he continued to go about the task as if he really knew what he was doing. There was one problem. He didn't know how much dynamite would be just right to do the job. It was pure and simple an estimate, a guesstimate.

When Hank was all set up, he breathed a prayer that he had enough dynamite packed under the stump and yet not so much it would blow it to kingdom come. The moment of truth came.

Hank glanced at the farmer with a knowing look of what he hoped came across as confidence and pushed down the plunger. The stump rose high in the air with a resounding boom and arched magnificently over toward his pickup truck and landed right on the roof of the cab, demolishing it.

The farmer turned to Hank and said, "Son, you didn't miss it by much — just a couple of feet. With a bit more practice you'll be able to land those suckers in the truck bed every time!"

Well, so much for experience and the old theme that practice makes perfect. There are lots of things in life for which we don't have the time to practice, and there are some moments when it is best just to act. Try this next story on for application.

A young man was busy at his job of sacking and carrying groceries out into the parking lot for the local supermarket. He had been in and out of the store on his helpful errands a number of times that morning. Something drew his attention to a woman in the parking lot who was struggling with her groceries. Her cart was filled, as were her arms.

His path back to the store took him in her direction. She put one of her packages on the roof of the car while she hunted for her keys. Then she began to load her packages from the cart to the car. But as she got in, started her car, and began to drive away, the young man saw her forgotten package on the roof. Now he was closer and began to run after the lady. When she made a turn to exit the parking lot, the package on the roof rolled off. Fortunately, the young man caught the package, a baby, before it hit the pavement!

Today's Quote: *We are saved by a person, and only by a person, and only by one person!* — William F. McDowell

Today's Verse: "Remain in me, and I will remain in you. No branch can bear fruit by itself; it must remain in the vine. Neither can you bear fruit unless you remain in me" (John 15:4).

It's in the Message

A young man was seeking a job as a "Morse code" operator. He found an ad in the local newspaper and went to the office address that was listed. He found it was a large, busy office with lots of hustle and bustle, including the constant chatter of a telegraph key in the background.

As he made his way into the office, a sign directed all the applicants for the position of telegraph operator to take a seat and wait until they were summoned into the inner office. About a dozen applicants were sitting, waiting ahead of him for their instructions. This was a bit discouraging, but the young man figured he had nothing to lose so he sat down along with the others to await his summons.

After two to three minutes this young man stood up, walked to the door where the sign was hanging and went right on through to the inner office. Naturally, all of the other applicants started looking at each other and muttering. After another five minutes the young man was back, this time with the employer. The employer looked at the dozen other applicants and said, "All of you gentlemen may go now. Thanks for your interest. The position has been filled by this young man."

At this, several of them grumbled again, and one of them spoke up and said, "Sir, I don't understand. He was the last one of us to come in, and we never even got a chance to be interviewed. Yet he got the job. I don't think that's really fair."

The employer said, "I'm sorry, but all the time you've been sitting here the telegraph key has been ticking out this message in Morse code: 'If you understand this message in Morse code, come right in. This job is yours.' None of you heard it. He did. The job is his!"

It's easy to become so absorbed in the moment that we fail to hear the still, small voice of God speaking to us. Are you so deafened by the roar of this world that the real message about Jesus Christ is being drowned out? Stop and listen to your heart. God may be speaking to you if you will only be open to hear His voice.

Today's Quote: *A sentence of death wonderfully concentrates the mind!* — Napoleon

Today's Verse: We preach Christ crucified: a stumbling block to Jews and foolishness to Gentiles, but to those whom God has called, both Jews and Greeks, Christ the power of God and the wisdom of God (1 Cor. 1:23–24).

Four steps to achievement:
Plan purposefully,
prepare prayerfully,
proceed positively,
pursue persistently.

William Arthur Ward (1812–1882)

The Soap Maker

Years ago a young man of sixteen left home to seek his fortune. All of his earthly possessions were tied up in a bundle. As he walked down the path, he met an old neighbor, the captain of a canal boat, and the following conversation took place.

"Well, William, where are you going?" the captain asked.

"I don't know," he answered. "My father is too poor to keep me at home any longer and says I must now make a living for myself."

"There's no trouble with that," said the captain. "Be sure you start right, and you'll get along fine."

William told his friend that the only trade he knew anything about was soap and candle making, at which he'd helped his father.

"Well," said the old man, "let me pray with you once more and give you a little advice, and then I'll let you go."

They both kneeled down on the tow path along which the horses walked as they pulled the boat in the canal. The man prayed and then gave his advice: "Someone will soon be the leading soap maker in New York. It can be you as well as anyone. I hope it may be. Be a good man, give your life totally to Christ, pay the Lord all that belongs to Him beginning with your tithe of every dollar you earn, make an honest soap, give a full pound, and I'm certain you will yet be a prosperous and rich man."

When young William arrived in the city, he found it hard to get work. Now lonesome and far from home, he remembered his mother's words and the last words of the canal boat captain. He was led to "seek first the kingdom of God and His righteousness," and became part of a growing church. He remembered his promise, and out of the first dollar he earned, he gave God His portion. He began with ten cents on the dollar. Finding regular employment, he soon became a partner in the business, and in a few years he became the sole owner.

He now resolved to keep his promise to the captain. He made an honest soap, gave a full pound, and instructed his bookkeeper to open an account with the Lord and place one-tenth of all company and personal earnings to that account.

He prospered, his business prospered, his family was blessed, his soap sold, and he grew richer faster than he had ever hoped. Soon he was giving it all to the Lord's work. Who was this soapmaker? William Colgate, today a household name.

Today's Quote: *Financial bondage is an immediate consequence of misunderstanding God's purposes for money!* — Bill Gothard

Today's Verse: Command those who are rich in this present world not to be arrogant nor to put their hope in wealth, which is so uncertain, but to put their hope in God, who richly provides us with everything for our enjoyment (1 Tim. 6:17).

Genius

There is nothing in his background to suggest that he might have been extraordinary. He was a bit less than an average student in school, and at times was a problem pupil. An incident occurred when he was fifteen years old and in high school. The teacher called Victor Seribriarkoff a "dunce!" That's not all — this teacher gave him the advice that it would be better if he dropped out of school and learned a trade.

Victor took that advice and acted upon it. He dropped out of school and for the next seventeen years went from job to job and became a wanderer, living life without a purpose and acting out the fact that he was a dunce.

At the age of thirty-two, however, something amazing took place! It was a moment that would change his life forever. Somehow, somewhere, somebody gave him an IQ test. The results? They revealed that he was a genius with an IQ of 161! Most of us are average with an IQ between 90 and 110.

From that moment, Victor Seribriarkoff began acting like the genius the IQ test indicated he was! Today he is quite a remarkable fellow. No longer is he a vagabond — he is a very successful businessman. He is the author of several books and has invented some new discoveries for which he holds the patents.

His name is not exactly a household word, but those who have heard of Victor know that he was elected to be the chairperson of the International Mensa Society. To belong to Mensa a person must have an IQ of 140 or above.

Once Victor realized who he really was, his entire life changed.

The way we see ourselves often determines what we become. Our self-image often develops from what other important people say about us. We listen to what they tell us, and then begin to act upon it. If we believe that we are a failure, then we act like a failure. If someone calls us a dunce and we believe that, we act like a dunce.

Today, my friend, do you really know who you are?

Think with me a moment or two about who you are. The Bible says you are God's greatest miracle! You are the salt of this earth and the light of this dark world. You have been given the secret of moving mountains. You are more precious than all this world's material things. You are rich, you are an overcomer, you are a child of the King of all kings! Act like who you are!

Today's Quote: *God don't make no junk!* — Ethel Waters

Today's Verse: For you created my inmost being; you knit me together in my mother's womb. I praise you because I am fearfully and wonderfully made . . . (Ps. 139:13–14).

Take Another Look

A shoe company in America sent two salesmen to an emerging, foreign country that was developing and moving into the twentieth century. The shoe manufacturer wanted to expand their market.

One of the salesmen returned home within two weeks. He was discouraged, giving up, and complaining, "You stupid guys sent me to a country where no one wears shoes!"

The other salesman stayed behind. He was not heard from for several weeks. Then a large package arrived crammed with orders for shoes of all sizes, types, and shapes. Included in this box of bulging orders was a hastily scrawled note that said, "Send me more order blanks! All the people here are barefoot, and everyone is a prospective customer!"

Perception is a tricky matter. In fact, it can be most illusive at times. Look at a glass of water that is exactly level at the middle. Will you describe it as being half-empty or half-full? It doesn't change the level of the water in the glass, but it does have a lot to do with your perspective.

Pull into a strange town or city and stop someone to ask directions to a particular destination. Invariably they will tell you, "Go to the third stoplight and turn left . . ." or something of the sort. Why not say, "Proceed to the first *go* light and . . . ." Stoplights spend as much time giving us the green light as they do displaying the red light. Why not call them "go lights?"

Listen to the next weather report on radio or television. The announcer will say, "Today is partly cloudy with a 30 percent change of rain." He could just as easily say, "Today is partly sunny with a 70 percent chance of no rain."

Too many of us have adopted a very pessimistic view of life. Do we see our communities as being so wicked that people are not interested in the message of the Church? Or do we see them as so needy they are waiting anxiously to be introduced to Jesus Christ?

Our perception of things can make or break us. Now this isn't a departure from reality that I am encouraging, but simply the idea that a correct perception and outlook will affect the way we approach life.

Jesus challenged the outlook of the disciples when He said, "Stop saying there are four months until harvest, look on the fields, they are white already for harvest." So take another look at your life situation. Does it still look impossible or can you see a breakthrough?

Today's Quote: *Success in life comes in cans, and failure comes in can'ts!* — Unknown

Today's Verse: Why art thou cast down, O my soul? and why art thou disquieted within me? hope in God: for I shall yet praise him, who is the health of my countenance, and my God (Ps. 43:5;KJV).

The Fruit of Kindness

It was a very nasty, stormy night at a small hotel in Philadelphia. An elderly man and woman approached the registration desk. Their question was, "Do you have room for us tonight?" Then, with a slight pause, the woman briefly explained, "We have been to some of the larger hotels, and they are all full."

The clerk explained that there were several conventions in town at the time, and indeed no rooms were available anywhere in Philadelphia that particular night. He also pointed out to them that all of the rooms in his hotel were full as well. But the clerk went on, "I wouldn't feel right about turning you out on such a nasty night. Would you be willing to sleep in my personal room?"

The couple was taken back at the generous offer and didn't know how to respond. The young man insisted that he would be able to get along just fine if only they would use his room.

The next day as the elderly couple was checking out, the man told the young clerk, "You are the kind of man who should be the boss of the best hotel in the country. Maybe someday I'll build one for you." They all smiled at the little joke, and then the clerk helped them carry their bags out to the street to load into their car.

Two years later, the clerk received a letter from the old man. He had almost forgotten the incident, but the letter recalled that night and his kindness. The letter also included a round trip ticket to New York City with the request that he come to be their guest for a visit.

When the young clerk reached New York City, there to meet him was the elderly couple. The old man drove him to the corner of Fifth Avenue and Thirty-fourth Street and pointed to a beautiful new building. It was like a palace of reddish stone with turrets and watchtowers like a castle. The older man said, "That is the hotel I have built for you to manage!"

"You must be joking," the young man said. He couldn't believe what he heard.

The old man said, "I'm not joking." And simply stood there and smiled.

The young man asked, "Who . . . who are you that you can do this?"

"My name is William Waldorf Astor." And the hotel was the original Waldorf-Astoria of New York City. The young clerk's name is George C. Boldt, and he did become the first manager of this historic hotel!

Today's Quote: *Neither genius, fame, nor love show the greatness of the soul. Only kindness can do that!* — Jean Baptiste Henri Lacordaire

Today's Verse: Love is patient, love is kind . . . (1 Cor. 13:4).

Little Things Matter

At age twenty-one, Jacques Lafitte, a son of a very poor carpenter of Bayonne, set out to seek his fortune and future life's work. He had no references from influential people, no brilliant academic career behind him, but he was young and full of hope. He arrived in Paris and with his usual thoroughness began looking for a job. Days became weeks, and still he had no job or income. But he kept at it. Nobody in Paris noticed this determined young man.

One morning Jacques applied at the office of a famous Swiss banker, Monsieur Perregaux. The banker asked him a few questions about himself, then he slowly shook his head and said there would be no job offered at the moment. Sadly, and more discouraged than ever, Jacques left the bank and walked across the courtyard. As he did so, he paused, stooped, and picked something up. Then he continued into the busy street, wondering if perhaps it wasn't time to return home.

At about that moment, he was overtaken by a man who tapped him on the shoulder. "Excuse me, sir," he said. "I'm an employee at the bank. Monsieur Perregaux wishes to see you again."

For the second time that morning Jacques faced the famous banker. "Pardon me," said Monsieur Perregaux, "but I happened to be watching you as you crossed the courtyard of the bank. You stooped and picked something up. Would you mind telling me what it was?"

"Only this," replied Jacques, wonderingly, as he took a bright new straight pin from the underside of the lapel of his coat.

"Aaah," exclaimed the banker, "THAT changes everything. We always have room here for anyone who is careful about little things. You may start at once." Thus, Jacques Lafitte began his long and amazingly successful association with the bank, ultimately assuming complete control of what became "Perregaux, Lafitte, and Company," one of the largest banks of Europe.

How many futures have hinged on such insignificant things? Little things are important in life and to God. Learn to pay attention to the little details of life, and you'll be amazed what this can lead to.

Today's Quote: *You can sit on a mountain but you cannot sit on a tack!* — Unknown

Today's Verse: There be four things which are little upon the earth, but they are exceeding wise: the ants . . . the conies . . . the locusts . . . the spider . . . (Prov. 30:24–28;KJV).

Gather ye rosebuds while ye may, old time is still a-flying, And this same flower that smiles today, tomorrow will be dying.

Robert Herrick (1591–1674)

The Power of Conviction

"Why are you bothering yourselves with a knitting machine?" asked Ari Davis of Boston, a manufacturer of instruments. "Why don't you make a sewing machine?" That particular question was overheard by a young man of twenty, Elias Howe.

No one took that question seriously, except the young Howe. It haunted him day and night until he resolved to produce one. He had an almost insane conviction that it could be done. Although he nearly starved in the process, some friends helped him to survive financially. Finally, in July of 1845, the machine was completed and proved its practicality by sewing the seams of two suits of woolen cloth! It could sew nearly three hundred stitches a minute. The mechanism was nearly perfect in this first attempt, and the sewing machine remains today, almost unchanged in design and mechanics — and all because of one man's conviction that it could be done!

Take the automobile. One man, Henry Ford, had the conviction that millions of cars could solve our transportation problems. He created the first assembly line for production, and the rest is history!

Samuel Morse had the conviction that electricity would carry a message over a wire! He was laughed at. Although Congress refused to appropriate the money to try the experiment, Morse held on to his conviction. He erected a wire between a hotel in Baltimore and a hotel in Washington, DC, and a United States senator heard the first message: "Behold what God hath wrought!"

When an idea grips a person with conviction, they will ultimately win against all kinds of odds.

What one thing can change your life around? What single obstacle stands behind the reality of progress? Truth becomes effective in your life by becoming a *conviction!*

Religious conviction is essential to spiritual success! The apostle Paul was invincible because he could say, "I know whom I have believed!"

The weakness of many a church pulpit today is due to the fact that the preacher has no strong convictions of the truth! Your life will remain weak and useless until you come to a place of conviction. Paul said, "I am persuaded . . ." which is another way of saying, "I have the conviction!"

Today's Quote: *The strength of a country is the strength of its religious convictions!* — Calvin Coolidge

Today's Verse: For I am persuaded, that neither death, nor life, nor angels, nor principalities, nor powers, nor things present, nor things to come, Nor height, nor depth, nor any other creature, shall be able to separate us from the love of God, which is in Christ Jesus our Lord (Rom. 8:38–39;KJV).

Premonitions

Over the past few decades, there has been a great deal of interest in the topic of prophecy.

One related topic of particular interest is that of premonitions. The following is an account of interest by Abraham Lincoln during his last days, as told to Ward Lamon and other guests at the White House, related in the book, *The Face of Lincoln*.

About ten days ago I retired very late. I could not have been long in bed when I fell into a slumber and soon began to dream. There seemed to be a death-like stillness about me. Then I heard subdued sobs, as if a number of people were weeping.

I wandered downstairs, but the mourners were invisible. I went from room to room, the same mournful sounds met me as I passed. I arrived at the East Room, which I entered. There I met a sickening surprise.

Before me was a catafalque, on which rested a corpse wrapped in funeral vestments. Around it were stationed soldiers who were acting as guards and there was a throng of people, some gazing mournfully upon the corpse, whose face was covered, others weeping pitifully.

"Who is dead in the White House?" I demanded of one of the soldiers.

"The president," was his answer. "He was killed by an assassin!"

Then came a loud burst of grief from the crowd, which awoke me from my dream. I slept no more that night, and although it was only a dream I have been strangely annoyed by it ever since.

Was Lincoln's dream a premonition or a prophecy? All of us want to have the privilege of looking into the future.

What would you do if you were to receive such a dream? Ignore it? Laugh at it? Act upon it? Or simply forget about it?

God does not always give us human beings an opportunity to look ahead. We are admonished to live a day at a time, making sure that we are ready to face death and the time of judgment that is to follow. What of your death? If you want to make heaven your eternal home, you must make an advance reservation.

Today's Quote: *God's finger touched him, and he slept!* — Alfred, Lord Tennyson

Today's Verse: Just as man is destined to die once, and after that to face judgment, so Christ was sacrificed once to take away the sins of many people . . . (Heb. 9:27–28).

Taking the Initiative

He was born in Columbus, Ohio, in 1890, the third of eight children. At age eleven he quit school to help with the family expenses and got his first, full-time job at $3.50 per week for a sixty-hour week.

At fifteen he became interested in automobiles and went to work in a garage at $4.50 per week. Knowing he would never get anywhere without more schooling, the teenager subscribed to a correspondence home study course on automobiles. Night after night, following long days at the garage, he worked at the kitchen table by the light of a kerosene lamp.

His next step was already planned in his mind. It was a job with the Frayer-Miller Automobile Company of Columbus. One day, when he felt he was ready and had prepared himself, he walked into the plant. Lee Frayer was bent over the hood of a car. The boy waited. Finally, Frayer noticed him. "Well," he said, "what do you want?"

"I just thought I'd tell you I'm coming to work here tomorrow," the boy replied with an air of confidence about him.

"Oh! Who hired you?" asked Frayer.

"Nobody yet, but I'll be on the job in the morning. If I'm not worth anything, you can fire me!"

Early the next morning, the young man returned to the garage. Frayer was not there yet. Noticing that the floor was thick with metal shavings and accumulated dirt and grease, the boy got a broom and shovel and set to work cleaning up the place.

The rest of this young man's future was predictable. He went on to a national reputation as a race car driver and automotive expert. During World War I, he was America's leading flying ace. Later he was the founder of Eastern Airlines. His name is, and you may well have guessed — Eddie Rickenbacker.

Initiative is defined in Random House Dictionary as "an introductory act or step; leading action; to take the initiative." It's an attitude that is sorely missing on the horizon of human endeavors. We live in a society that wants everything in life handed to them on a silver platter.

The same thinking holds true in Christian living. We want it all done for us so all we have to do is enjoy the final result. How about beginning a revival of good old fashioned initiative in our living? Long live initiative!

Today's Quote: *Hungry man sit long time with mouth open waiting for roast duck to fly in !* — Old Chinese Proverb

Today's Verse: For even when we were with you, we gave you this rule: "If a man will not work, he shall not eat." We hear that some among you are idle. They are not busy; they are busybodies (2 Thess. 3:10–11).

The Ugly Pet

A young boy and his family moved from a small southern town to a large metropolitan area in the northeastern United States. The young boy was very unhappy with the move for he had to leave behind all his friends. Beside, he knew he was going to hate big-city life. The one bright spot for the boy was that he had been allowed to bring his pet.

After moving into their new home, the boy and his pet went for a walk to see the neighborhood. As they strolled across a school yard, they were suddenly face to face with a local gang. The leader looked at the boy and said, "So you're the new kid in town. If you plan to live here, you have to join a gang and it better be mine!"

The boy told him, "We didn't have gangs where I came from, and I don't think it'd be right for me to join."

The bully responded, "You don't have a choice." Just then he noticed for the first time the boy's pet and began to laugh. "Look at that ugly dog. That is the ugliest thing I ever saw! Yellow, beady-eyed, short-tailed, long-nosed, short-legged ugly dog! What kind of a dog is it? Never mind, I tell you what I'm going to do. If you don't join my gang by tomorrow evening, I'm going to have my dog Killer rip up that ugly yellow, beady-eyed, short-tailed, long-nosed, stumpy-legged dog of yours to shreds. You be here tomorrow night or else!"

The boy said, "I'll be here, but I don't think I'll join your gang."

The next evening the boy and his pet were there at the school yard. Sure enough here came the gang, and one of them was holding onto a chain hooked to Killer, a German Shepherd about three feet high at the shoulders. With his enormous, slavering mouth full of large teeth, Killer was straining to get at that ugly yellow dog. The gang leader released Killer, "Get 'em, Killer!"

Killer circled a couple of times, then jumped in on that ugly creature. In the middle of its jump, the boy's pet opened the largest mouth the gang had ever seen and in one bite killed Killer! The gang was shocked!

Finally, the gang leader asked the boy, "What kind of dog is that ugly yellow, short-tailed, long-nosed, beady-eyed, stumpy-legged thing anyway?"

"Well," the boy replied, "before we cut his tail off and painted him yellow, he was an alligator!"

Yes, my friend, appearances can be deceiving. Watch out, today!

Today's Quote: *Ever hear about the cross-eyed discus thrower? He didn't set any records but he sure kept the crowd awake!* — Unknown

Today's Verse: Be sober, be vigilant; because your adversary the devil, as a roaring lion, walketh about, seeking whom ever he may devour (1 Pet. 5:8;KJV).

"I'll Be That Man"

February is a unique month on our calendar. It's the only month that will vary in the number of days. Every fourth year it has an extra day, the twenty-ninth. But it's also unique in that it commemorates the birthdays of famous men: Abraham Lincoln, St. Valentine, and George Washington. Let's add to that another great man: Dwight Lyman Moody, whose birthday is on February 5.

Moody grew up in the tiny town of Northfield, Massachusetts, on the bank of the Connecticut River six miles south of the New Hampshire-Vermont border. With less than a high school education, the seventeen-year-old Dwight headed for Boston to make his way in a bigger world. He succeeded as a shoe salesman but far more as a soul winner! Denied membership in one church because of his ignorance of the Bible, he rented a pew in another and filled it with street people. Moody proved tireless in his efforts to see people put their trust in Jesus Christ. His approach was simple and most direct.

"Are you a Christian?" he would ask.

Unless the prospect could respond promptly with a convincing answer, he would find Moody in quick pursuit. "Why not?"

Moody's reputation spread. One day on a street in Chicago a stranger handled Moody's stock question with a sharp retort: "That's none of your business!"

"Oh, yes, it is!" Moody snapped back.

The man eyed him warmly. "Then you must be D.L. Moody."

Perhaps the turning point of his life happened when he was a young man. A friend, whose name is unknown, said to Moody, "The world has yet to see what God can do with a man totally committed to Him."

Moody is reported to have thought a moment and then exclaimed, "By God's grace, I'll be that man!"

As a result of his life and vision, more than twenty-three thousand former Moody students minister full-time across the United States and in other countries around the world. Nearly six thousand alumni missionaries' names appear in the foyer of the Moody Bible Institute's auditorium. Twenty of these have been martyred for their faith in Jesus Christ!

Today's Quote: *By God's grace, I'll be that man!* — D.L. Moody

Today's Verse: They that be wise shall shine as the brightness of the firmament; and they that turn many to righteousness as the stars for ever and ever (Dan. 12:3;KJV).

Faith is greater than learning.

Martin Luther

Going Home to Roost

John L. Smith was a loyal and hard working carpenter who had worked for the same very successful contractor for many years. John was the kind of man whom any employer would be pleased to employ.

One day the contractor called John into his office and said, "John, I'm putting you completely in charge of the next house we build. I want you to order all the materials and oversee the entire job!"

John accepted the assignment with great enthusiasm and excitement. Here was his big break! For ten days before the ground was broken at the building site, John studied the blueprints. He checked every measurement, every cut, every specification. Suddenly he had a thought: "If I am really in charge, why couldn't I cut a few corners, use less expensive materials and put the extra money into my pocket? Who would know the difference? Once the house is finished and painted, it will look just great."

So John carefully laid out his scheme. He ordered second-grade lumber, but his reports indicated that it was top-grade. He ordered inexpensive concrete for the foundation and used the very cheapest sub-contractors on the job. All the while, he reported higher figures than were quoted. He had the least expensive wiring put in that would pass the inspector's close watch. Cutting corners in materials as well as in construction, John continued to report the purchase of the best materials. Soon the home was finished, landscaped, and painted. He asked the contractor to come by and see the finished product.

The contractor walked through the house, stopped in the kitchen, turned to John L. Smith, loyal employee, and said, "John, what a magnificent job you have done! You have been such a good and faithful employee all these years in my firm that I have decided it's time to show my gratitude to you and your family. I am giving you this house you have built, as my gift!"

There are no easy short-cuts in life! There is no way that you can just barely get by, especially when it comes to laying foundational truths into your own personal life. If the foundation is strong and built with the best of materials, it allows the structure erected upon it to also stand the test of time. Cutting corners, using shoddy materials, taking the easy way out always, eventually, leads to disaster. At some point in life, all of us must pay our dues.

We, who are followers of the Carpenter of Nazareth, are called upon to study, read, apply, pray, and live in obedience — this is a life well constructed.

Today's Quote: *A diamond is a chunk of coal that made good under pressure!* — Classic Crossword Puzzles

Today's Verse: For we are taking pains to do what is right, not only in the eyes of the Lord but also in the eyes of men (2 Cor. 8:21).

A True Sportsman

The Olympic Games of 1936 were hosted in Hitler's Germany. The American entry in the running broad jump was Jesse Owens, a black athlete. Luz Long, a blond, blue-eyed athlete who had trained all his life for this event, represented Germany. Hitler desperately wanted Long to win to support his propaganda for the "master" race.

In the trials, Jesse Owens did badly. He had to jump a qualifying distance of 24'-6" but failed in his first attempt. Luz Long qualified easily. Then Owens, being extra cautious on his second attempt, fell three inches short of the qualifying distance. Owens was now extremely nervous. Before his third and final try, he rested on one knee attempting to pray.

Then someone called his name and put a calm, reassuring hand on his shoulder. It was Luz Long! "I think I know what is wrong with you," said Luz, seconds before Owens was to jump. "You give everything when you jump. I the same. You cannot do halfway, but you are afraid you will foul again."

"That's right," said Jesse.

"I have the answer," said Luz. "The same thing happened to me last year in Cologne." Luz told Owens to jump half a foot behind the takeoff board, using full power. That way it was possible not to foul and yet not hold back. Luz then put his towel down at the exact spot from which Jesse should jump.

It worked. Jesse qualified, setting an unofficial world record. Thanks to Luz, America's black man was still in the running.

The day of the finals, Luz jumped first, and Jesse jumped a bit further. Luz's second jump outdid Jesse's first; Jesse then jumped a half inch farther. Luz outdid himself on his third try, setting a new world record.

Now it was Jesse Owens' final turn. Before he took off, he caught Luz Long's eye. He said later he felt that his opponent was "wordlessly urging me to do my best, to do better than I'd ever done."

And Jesse did. Luz had set a new world record, and Jesse jumped farther! "You did it!" said Luz. Then he held Jesse's arm up in the air. "Jazze Owenz! Jazze Owenz!" he shouted to the crowd, and soon one hundred thousand Germans were chanting with him, "Jazze Owenz!"

Luz failed to prove Hitler's theory of the master race and instead proved himself to be one of the finest sportsman of all time.

Today's Quote: *Maturity is the ability to do a job whether or not you are supervised, to carry money without spending it, and to bear an injustice without wanting to get even!* — Ann Landers

Today's Verse: I do not run like a man running aimlessly; I do not fight like a man beating the air. No, I beat my body and make it my slave . . . (1 Cor. 9:26–27).

Life and Accountability

Grand Admiral Karl Doenitz — Adolf Hitler's personally appointed successor who presided over Nazi Germany's unconditional surrender in World War II — died in 1980 in Hamburg at the age of eighty-nine. A West German Defense Ministry spokesman said that Doenitz, who commanded Germany's U-boat campaign against Allied shipping, was buried without military honors. Why? The ministry, fearing pro-Nazi demonstrations, had also banned any soldiers from attending the funeral in uniform.

Doenitz, a brilliant submarine strategist, was appointed by Hitler as his successor on April 30, 1945. In that role he presided over Germany's surrender after a futile attempt to surrender in the West, and Doenitz continued to fight on against the Russians in the East.

After Hitler notified Doenitz that he was to succeed him as head of state, the Nazi leader committed suicide the same day. In fact, Doenitz had been exercising supreme authority for some days since Hitler had become so overwrought he had been unable to make decisions. Doenitz was arrested by the British on May 22, 1945.

Karl Doenitz, slightly built and taciturn, was imprisoned for ten years after his conviction for war crimes at the Nuremberg trials in 1947. His was the lightest sentence given to any of the major war criminals convicted at the Nuremberg trials. After completing his sentence, he was released from Berlin's Spandau Prison on October 1, 1956.

The admiral's memoirs, published in 1959, attempted to refute the Nuremberg verdict in his case, maintaining, as did many other Nazis, that he was following military orders. He said he was shocked when, at the war's end, he learned of the atrocities committed by Hitler.

What does a story like this say to us today? One of the first lessons is that every one of us is responsible for our life actions, and we will be held accountable for them. This applies to all people, whether you have been a world leader, a decorated war hero, or just an average Joe. We all must face the inevitability of death, which in turn will be followed by a judgment.

How can we prepare for such an event? One thing is positively certain — you can make no further preparations after you have died. This fact calls forth from all of us a consciousness of an eternity for which we must prepare!

Today's Quote: *There is no fear of judgment for the man who judges himself according to the Word of God!* — Howard G. Hendricks

Today's Verse: And as it is appointed unto men once to die, but after this the judgment: So Christ was once offered to bear the sins of many (Heb. 9:27–28;KJV).

Lessons from Salesmen

The sales manager was complaining to his secretary about one of his men: "Harry has such a bad memory; it's a wonder he remembers to breathe. I asked him to pick up a newspaper on his way back from lunch, but I'm not even sure he'll remember his way back to the office."

Just then Harry burst in the door, brimming with excitement and exclaimed: "Guess what, boss! At lunch I ran into old man Jones who hasn't given us an order in seven years. Before he left, I talked him into a multi-million-dollar contract!"

The sales manager sighed and looked at his secretary, "What did I tell you? He forgot the newspaper!"

Now there's a man who has his priorities turned around.

Another story tells about a young salesman who asked the receptionist for an appointment to see the company's sales manager. Ushered into the office, the young salesman said, "I don't suppose you want to buy any life insurance, now, do you?"

"No," replied the sales manager curtly.

"I didn't think so," said the salesman dejectedly, gathering up his briefcase as he got up to leave.

"Wait a minute," said the sales manager. "I want to talk to you." The salesman sat down again, obviously nervous and confused.

"I train salesmen," said the sales manager, "and you're about the worst I've seen yet. You'll never sell anything until you show a little confidence and accentuate the positive. You just have to get with it and be sold on your product. Now, because you're obviously new at this, I'll help you out by signing up for a fifty-thousand dollar policy."

After the sales manager had signed on the dotted line, he said helpfully, "You are going to have to develop a few standard organized sales talks."

"Oh, but I have," replied the salesman with a big smile. "This is my standard organized sales talk just for sales managers! It works every time!"

Jesus stated that many times the people of this world are wiser than are the children who make up the kingdom of God. Innovation, creativity, and a new approach are too many times foreign to the people who make up the Church. It's time for us to be creative in our witness and ministry to this world! Go for it!

Today's Quote: *The Lord gives us friends to push us to our potential . . . And enemies to push us beyond it!* — Jim Vorsas

Today's Verse: "I am sending you out like sheep among wolves. Therefore be as shrewd as snakes and as innocent as doves. Be on your guard against men . . ." (Matt. 10:16–17).

Keep Going

The setting was a cold January morning in a little town in Northern Wisconsin on the southern shore of Lake Superior. It happened to be a Saturday when the town had their annual dog-sled race on the lake. A one-mile course had been staked out by sticking little fir trees in the ice. Because of the steep slope of the shore, those standing above the ice could easily view the entire course.

It was a youngster's meet, and the contenders ranged all the way from large boys with several dogs and big sleds to one little fellow, who was about six years old, with a tiny little sled and one dog.

They all took off at the signal, and soon the little fellow with his single dog was quickly outdistanced. He was so far behind it seemed as though he wasn't even in the race or was running one by himself.

All went well until — about half-way around — the team that was in second place started to pass the team then in the lead. In the excitement of the race, the driver of the second-place team guided his dogs too close to the lead team, and the dogs got into a fight.

Then as each team came up, the dogs joined in the fight. None of the young drivers could seem to steer their dogs and sleds around the melee. Soon, the race had turned into a seething mass of dogs fighting, snapping, charging, growling, tumbling, and barking — all tangled up in sleds, boys, and harnesses!

The drivers of those sleds were in the middle, striking out at dogs, hitting, and trying to pull them apart! Whistling and shouting, the boys pulled with all their strength to free their full-grown, angry and growling Alaskan huskies. It was a total mess.

From the position of the spectators, what was once a race appeared to be just one huge, black seething mass of kids, sleds, and dogs.

Then they could see that little fellow with the little sled and the very little dog closing in on the fight. He simply guided his dog around the jumbled pile — the only one to manage it. He crossed the finish line amid the cheering of the crowd, taking the first place and making him the only winner! When he was interviewed at the finish line, he was asked how he did it. His reply was simple: "I just kept on going and kept my dog from getting into the fight. That's all!"

Today's Quote: *No matter how difficult the challenge or how hopeless the task, if you are on course, just keep on going!*

Today's Verse: All men will hate you because of me, but he who stands firm to the end will be saved (Matt. 10:22).

If you think education is expensive — try ignorance.

Derek Bok

Choices

This is a story about a man named Joe who inherited a million dollars. The will, however, provided that he had to accept it either in Chile or Brazil. He chose Brazil. Unhappily it turned out that in Chile he would have received his inheritance in land on which uranium, gold, and silver had just been discovered.

Once in Brazil, he had to choose between receiving his inheritance in coffee or nuts. He chose nuts. Too bad! The bottom fell out of the nut market, and coffee went up to $1.50 per pound, wholesale. Poor Joe lost everything he had to his name.

He went out and sold his gold watch for the money he needed to fly back home. It seems that he had enough for a ticket to either New York or Boston. He chose Boston. When the plane for New York taxied up, he noticed it was a brand-new 747 super-jet with all the latest technology. The plane for Boston arrived, and it was a 1928 old Ford tri-motor with a sway back. It was filled with crying children and tethered goats and sheep. It seemed like it took all day to get off the runway.

Over the Andes, one of the engines fell off. Our man Joe made his way to the captain and said, "I'm a jinx on this plane. Let me out if you want to save your lives. Give me a parachute."

The pilot agreed, but added, "On this plane, anybody who bails out must wear two parachutes."

So Joe jumped out of the plane. As he fell through the air, he tried to make up his mind which ripcord to pull. Finally, he chose the one on the left. It was rusty, and the wire pulled loose. So he pulled the other handle. This chute opened, but its shroud line snapped. In desperation, Joe cried out, "St. Francis, save me!"

A hand reached out of heaven and grabbed the poor man by the wrist and let him dangle in mid-air. Then a gentle but inquisitive voice asked, "St. Francis Xavier or St. Francis of Assisi?"

Choices! Choices! I had a person tell me one day, "Life would be just great if I weren't confronted with so many choices."

My friend, life is nothing more or less than a series of choices. It's a fantastic power that has been given to each human being. Use this power well. It's called choice!

Today's Quote: *Three choices every person needs to make right: Master, mission, and mate!* — Eleanor Doan

Today's Verse: And if it seem evil unto you to serve the Lord, choose you this day whom ye will serve; whether the gods which your fathers served that were on the other side of the flood, or the gods of the Amorites, in whose land ye dwell: but as for me and my house, we will serve the Lord (Josh. 24:15;KJV).

A Loser?

When he was a little boy, the other children called him "Sparky" after a comic-strip horse named Sparkplug. Sparky never shook that nickname. School was all but impossible for Sparky. He failed every subject in the eighth grade. Every subject! In high school, he flunked physics by receiving a flat zero in the course. Sparky distinguished himself as the worst physics student in his school's history.

He also flunked Latin. And algebra. And English. He didn't do much better in sports. Although he managed to make the school golf team, he promptly lost the only important match of the year. There was a consolation match, but Sparky lost that, too.

Throughout his youth, Sparky was awkward socially. He was not actually disliked by the other youngsters, it's just that no one cared that much. If a classmate ever said hello to him outside of school hours, Sparky was astonished. There was no way to tell how he might have done at dating since, in high school, Sparky never once asked a girl out. He was too afraid of being turned down.

Sparky was a loser. He, his classmates, everyone knew it to be true. So he rolled with it. He would be content with the inevitable mediocrity.

But, there's more to Sparky: drawing. He was proud of his own artwork. Of course, no one else appreciated it. In his senior year of high school, he submitted some cartoons to the editors of the class yearbook. Almost predictably, Sparky's drawings were rejected.

He decided to become a professional artist. After graduation he wrote to Walt Disney Studios telling of his qualifications to become a cartoonist for Disney. He received a form letter requesting some samples of his work. Sparky waited for the reply, but deep down he knew that, too, would be rejected, which it was.

So what did Sparky do? He wrote his autobiography in cartoons. He described his childhood self — the little-boy loser, the chronic underachiever — in a cartoon the whole world now knows.

The boy who failed the eighth grade, the young artist whose work was rejected by Walt Disney and his own yearbook staff is known to us today as "Sparky" Charles Monroe Schulz. He created the "Peanuts" comic strip and the cartoon character whose kite would never fly — CHARLIE BROWN!

Today's Quote: *"How did the other team feel?"* (The question asked by Charlie Brown on being told by Linus of an unbelievable ballgame, won on a last minute touchdown, by Charles Monroe Schulz.)

Today's Verse: "All men will hate you because of me, but he who stands firm to the end will be saved" (Matt. 10:22).

Day 22
One Huge Hamburger

Maybe you have already heard about the world's largest hamburger. If not, or even if you have, I'm going to tell you about it anyway. It weighed in at 3,591 pounds. It was created by the people of Rutland, North Dakota, and was cooked on a Saturday afternoon barbecue back in July of 1982.

Yes, it was a single hunk of meat that measured 2-1/2 inches thick and 16 feet across. The meat was provided by local farmers. It was cooked on one of the largest griddles you can imagine. The griddle was made of a 201-square-foot steel plate that was heated by 1.5 million BTUs of propane. It must have been quite some contraption.

The hamburger patty was brought from a processing plant via refrigerated truck. On the way to the barbecue, the patty was weighed at the local grain elevator, beating the former world record (set by the people in Perth, Australia) by a total of 332 pounds. The new record now stands in the Guinness Book of World Records, I suppose under the "foods" category.

The mayor of Rutland, Ronald Narum, said it was the biggest thing to hit his little town since the town burned down three years previously. The big cookout was part of the centennial festivities for the small town nestled in the southeastern part of North Dakota.

It took two hours of cooking to get the huge hamburger ready to eat. They then cut it into sixty-five hundred patties and served it to approximately six thousand people who were present for the event. I suppose they could all brag about having had a bite of the world's largest sandwich.

I can tell you, though, that each of those six thousand people got hungry again the next day! Even a good-sized bite from the world's largest hamburger can't keep a person from getting hungry again.

Everybody has a hunger, but it's a hunger for something more than the world's biggest or best. It's a hunger to know God. Every person has been created with a "God-shaped vacuum" inside, which only He can satisfy. We live in a world that strives to satisfy its hunger for God with all kinds of bogus meals, none of which does the trick. The answer is not in pleasure, food, possessions, money, power, fame, or self-satisfaction. It's in a personal relationship with an eternal loving God.

Jesus talked about food and the satisfaction that there is only in Him. Taste and see that the Lord is good!

Today's Quote: *A laugh is worth a hundred groans in any market!* — Unknown

Today's Verse: Then Jesus declared, "I am the bread of life. He who comes to me will never go hungry, and he who believes in me will never be thirsty" (John 6:35).

Horses and Water

Joseph Duveen is known as one of the world's finest art dealers. During his career, his client list read like the who's who in society and collecting. But there was one not named among his clientele, and Duveen was not content to rest until he had Andrew Mellon, the most discriminating art collector of all, to add to his list. In order to entice Mr. Mellon, Joseph Duveen carefully laid out a plan.

Patiently, over a number of years, Duveen put together a superlative collection of old masters' paintings with which he would tempt this discriminating collector. Finally, he was ready to make his move.

Duveen had his name put on the waiting list in order to lease the apartment directly beneath Mr. Mellon's in Washington, DC. He waited patiently for the call that eventually came telling of the now vacant apartment. After having each painting exquisitely framed, Duveen went to the apartment and hung the carefully selected collection from the old masters, literally covering the walls.

Then, before he returned to New York, Duveen offered the key to his apartment to Andrew Mellon and said, "Mr. Mellon, you are invited, anytime you might like, to drop in and look at the paintings." He encouraged him to feel free to view them whenever he desired.

Mr. Mellon's curiosity drew him to the pictures and the apartment. After the first visit, the financier could not stay away. He came back to the apartment night after night, and he would stay for hours admiring the pictures of the old masters. This went on for a few weeks with Mellon coming back each night for another look at the paintings.

Finally a call went to Joseph Duveen in New York asking if it would be possible for him to return to Washington. When that meeting took place in the apartment, Andrew Mellon proposed the purchase of the entire collection. This was a staggering transaction for Duveen who received $2 million for his paintings and Mellon as his new client!

All of us have heard the old adage that you can lead a horse to water, but you can't make him drink. But it is possible to salt the horse's hay a little to encourage the drinking to take place!

Jesus said, "No man can come to me, except the Father which has sent me draw him . . ." (John 6:44;KJV). God loves you enough to keep inviting you to accept His Son as your Saviour. What are you waiting for? The gift of eternal life is worth far more than any treasures this world has to offer.

Today's Quote: *Rich isn't just a state of mind. It's not having to arrange your vacation so that you arrive home on pay day!* — Funny, Funny World

Today's Verse: Again, the kingdom of heaven is like unto a merchant man, seeking goodly pearls: Who, when he had found one pearl of great price, went and sold all that he had, and bought it (Matt. 13:45–46;KJV).

Getting What You Want

A man lived in a squalid tenement on a side street in East Boston. As a tailor, he worked long hours each day to barely eke out a meager existence. But he allowed himself one luxury: one ticket each year to the Irish Sweepstakes. And each year he would pray fervently that this would be the winning ticket that would bring him good fortune.

For fourteen years, his life continued in the same impoverished vein, until one day there came a loud knocking at his door. Two well-dressed gentlemen entered his shop and informed him that he had just won the Irish Sweepstakes! The grand prize was $500,000!

The little tailor could hardly believe his ears! He was rich! No longer would he have to slave away making pant cuffs, hemming dresses, shortening sleeves. Now he could really begin to live! He locked up his shop and threw the key into the Charles River. He bought himself a wardrobe fit for a king, a new Rolls Royce, a suite of rooms at the Ritz, and soon was supporting a string of attractive women.

Night after night he partied until dawn, spending his money as if each day was his last. Of course the inevitable happened. One day the money was all gone. Furthermore, he had nearly wrecked his health.

Disillusioned, ridden with fever and exhausted, he returned to his little shop and set up business once more. Fom force of habit, once again each year he set aside the price of an Irish Sweepstakes ticket.

Two years later, there again came a knock at his door. The same two gentlemen stood there once again. "This is the most incredible thing in the history of the Irish Sweepstakes," exclaimed one. "You have won again! Your grand prize is another $500,000!"

The little tailor staggered to his feet with a groan that could be heard by people outside his shop. "Oh, no!" he protested. "Do you mean I have to go through all that all over again?"

Getting what you want may be just as difficult to handle as having nothing in the first place. Too many people have found that living with success is much more testing than living in failure. One of the most overlooked Christian principles is to learn to be content with what we have and where we are. Dissatisfaction can drive you to real distraction.

Today's Quote: *Be careful, or you may get what you want!* — Old Saying

Today's Verse: I am not saying this because I am in need, for I have learned to be content whatever the circumstances (Phil. 4:11).

The lure of the distant and difficult is deceptive. The great opportunity is where you are.

John Burroughs (1837–1921)

Because of Trouble

About the turn of the century, young Clarence took his girlfriend for an outing and picnic at a nearby lake. He was typically dressed in a suit with a tight, high collar. She wore a long dress with about a dozen petticoats and carried a parasol. As Clarence rowed laboriously in the hot sun, his young lady friend relaxed beneath the shade of her parasol, looking sweet and feminine. As he rowed, he drank in the aroma of her perfume.

Despite the hot sun and the sweat on his face, Clarence became hypnotized by his girlfriend's beauty as he watched her smile. They finally reached their destination, a small island in the center of the lake. Clarence dragged the boat onto the shore and then helped his girlfriend out of the boat.

After he placed their picnic beneath a spreading shade tree, she began speaking to him in soft whispers. He loved her voice and listened intently.

She whispered, "Clarence, honey, you forgot the ice cream."

"Ice cream," muttered Clarence, finally remembering that they'd planned on ice cream for the dessert. He got back into the boat and rowed to shore. He found a grocery store, bought the ice cream, and made his way back across the lake. He got out of the boat and trudged up to the shade of the tree.

She looked at the ice cream, batted long eyelashes over her deep blue eyes and purred, "Honey, you forgot the chocolate syrup."

Love makes people do strange things. So, Clarence got into the boat, rowed across the lake, went to the same grocery store, bought the chocolate syrup, returned to the boat, and began to row in the steaming, afternoon sun. He rowed about halfway across and stopped. He sat there for the rest of the afternoon thinking that there must be a much better way. By the end of that hot, summer afternoon, Clarence Evinrude had invented the outboard motor!

Before you come to the conclusion that this is fiction, just check the history of the Evinrude outboard motor. In the first four months of their advertising campaign for the new outboard motor, this story was told as the origin of the idea. Oh, yes, Clarence later married the girl he had left stranded on the island for an afternoon.

Most of this world's discoveries and inventions have come out of times of trouble and need. Why? Because there are people who look for opportunity in the worst kind of situations. When you cultivate the attitude of looking for opportunity out of adversity, you, too, will find success in life.

Today's Quote: *Necessity is the mother of invention!* — Unknown

Today's Verse: Answer me when I call to you, O my righteous God. Give me relief from my distress; be merciful to me and hear my prayer (Ps. 4:1).

Missed Opportunities

This is the story of a man who had a fantastic opportunity — which he missed. One day a friend took him for a ride way out into the country. They drove off the main road and through a grove of trees to a large uninhabited expanse of land. A few horses were grazing, and a couple of old shacks remained standing.

The friend, Walter, stopped the car, got out, and started to describe with great vividness the wonderful things he was going to build. And he wanted his friend, Arthur, to buy some of the land surrounding his project to get in on the ground floor.

But Arthur thought to himself, *Who in the world is going to drive 25 miles for this crazy project? The logistics of the venture are staggering.*

And so Walter explained to his friend Arthur, "I can handle the main project myself. But it will take all my money. The land bordering it, where we're standing now, will in just a couple of years be jammed with hotels and restaurants and convention halls to accommodate the people who will come to spend their entire vacations here at my park."

Walter continued, "I want you to have the first chance at this surrounding acreage because in the next five years it will increase in value several hundred times."

"What could I say? I knew he was wrong," Arthur tells the story today. "I knew he had let a dream get the best of his common sense, so I mumbled something about a tight money situation and promised that I would look into the whole thing a little later on."

"Later on will be too late," Walter cautioned Arthur as they walked back to the car. "You'd better move on it right now."

And so Art Linkletter turned down the opportunity to buy up all the land that surrounded what was to become Disneyland. His friend Walt Disney had tried to talk him into it, but Art thought he was crazy.

The rest is history! California's Disneyland is today one of the major attractions for tourists in America. Can you imagine what the land surrounding this theme park is worth today?

Have you ever been presented with a one-time opportunity? I think all of us have had or know about friends who turned down a once-in-a-lifetime opportunity only to live to regret it later.

Take another look at the opportunity to serve the Lord with your life.

Today's Quote: *The door of opportunity is so wide open that it's off its hinges!* — Ernie Reb

Today's Verse: Therefore, as we have opportunity, let us do good to all people, especially to those who belong to the family of believers (Gal. 6:10).

Turning a Disadvantage

With the presses all set to run three million copies of Theodore Roosevelt's 1912 convention speech, the publisher found permission had not been obtained to use photos of Roosevelt and his running mate, Governor Hiram Johnson of California. Copyright laws at that time put the penalty for such oversights at one dollar per copy! They were faced with a seemingly insurmountable problem! Time was at a premium.

The chairman of the campaign committee was equal to the situation. He dictated a telegram to the Chicago studio that had taken the pictures, and it read like this: "Planning to issue three million copies of Roosevelt speech with pictures of Roosevelt and Johnson on cover. Great publicity opportunity for photographers. What will you pay us to use your photographs?"

An hour later the reply was wired back: "Appreciate opportunity, but can pay only $250."

That particular chairman displayed various traits of exciting leadership. He showed himself to be cool under fire. He didn't let what might have boggled the mind of a lesser man affect his thinking process. And he made the best of a bad situation that had all the earmarks of a disaster in the making.

Often in life when something goes wrong and appears to bring with it devastating consequences, there is a very human tendency to be overwhelmed. This in turn can lead to a sort of mental paralysis that results in no action being taken. Imagine where this country would be if all our leadership became paralyzed when faced with a problem.

When things go sour, remember to keep your wits about you. If you do, you may be able to think your way out of trouble. Or at the very least be able to lessen the blow.

Instead of allowing yourself the luxury of over-reacting, consider calmly the crisis you face; then consider the alternatives. Ask for help from a person or persons whose trusted knowledge and character you respect. Sometimes the cold shower of truth will bail you out. If worse comes to worst, don't attempt to cover it up, but face the situation squarely.

When you really become accomplished at handling the disadvantages of life or the negatives, you may even graduate to the point where you'll be able to turn them into advantages or positives!

Today's Quote: *Stormy weather is what man needs from time to time to remind him he's not really in charge of anything!* –– Bill Vaughn

Today's Verse: In all thy ways acknowledge him, and he shall direct thy paths (Prov. 3:6;KJV).

Be Thankful

For a number of years, the Northwestern University, located in Evanston, Illinois, had maintained a volunteer life-saving crew, recruited from its student body. In actuality, this group became quite famous and well-known for their heroics on Lake Michigan.

The story goes that on September 8, 1860, the *Lady Elgin,* a crowded passenger steamer, foundered and ran aground. As it began breaking apart on the rocks off the shore of the lake just above Evanston, a crowd soon gathered.

One of the students, Edward W. Spencer, who was attending the Garrett Biblical Institute (a part of Northwestern), was a member of the volunteer life-saving crew. He spotted a woman hanging on to some of the wreckage out in the breakers and threw off his coat to swim out through the heavy waves to rescue her, which he was successful in doing.

Fifteen more times, on this day, the young and brave Spencer swam out into the treacherous water to save a total of seventeen persons. Following his last rescue attempt, he collapsed in a heap on the shore. He was totally exhausted!

Recovery from the total giving of himself on that day was a slow process. Exposure and exertion had taken their toll. In fact, he never completely recovered. His health was broken so completely that he had to drop out of the Bible institute, and his dream of entering the ministry was over. He lived the rest of his life in isolated seclusion, hoarding his fragile health. His life, marked by his devotion to the Lord Jesus Christ, was a living example of what Christianity is all about. He moved to California for health reasons and lived there until he died at the age of eighty-one.

In the simple notice of his death that appeared in the local paper, it was mentioned that not one of those seventeen persons he had rescued ever came to thank him or wrote him or in any way expressed gratitude!

Samuel Liebowits, an attorney who has specialized in snatching killers from the death chambers, notes that — of the seventy-eight men he has been able to save from the electric chair — not one ever sent him as much as a Christmas card or note of thanks.

Even Jesus bore the disservice of ingratitude from the people He healed. Let's give thanks, always!

Today's Quote: *A thankful heart is not only the greatest virtue, but the parent of all the other virtues!* — Unknown

Today's Verse: But mark this: There will be terrible times in the last days. People will be lovers of themselves, lovers of money, boastful, proud, abusive, disobedient to their parents, ungrateful, unholy (2 Tim. 3.1–2).

Right of Way

An officer in the U.S. Navy had always dreamed of commanding a battleship. He had graduated from the Naval Academy, worked hard, studied diligently to make his new ranks, and been a good officer. Although he had a touch of arrogance and pride in his make-up, it was not enough to hinder his steady climb to a command.

He finally achieved that dream and was given commission of the newest and proudest battleship in the navy. What a lofty moment! He had made it!

One very stormy night, as the battleship was making its way through the choppy seas, the captain was on duty on the bridge surveying his proud world. Off the port side, he spotted a strange light rapidly closing with his own ship. Immediately, he ordered the signalman to flash this message to the unidentified craft: "Alter your course 10 degrees to the south."

It was just a minute or two before the reply came: "Alter your course 10 degrees to the north."

Determined that *his* battleship would not take a back seat to another vessel, the captain snapped out this order to be sent: "Alter your course 10 degrees to the south — I am the CAPTAIN!"

The response was beamed right back: "Alter your course 10 degrees to the south — I am Seaman Third Class Jones."

At this reply, the captain was now infuriated. He grabbed the signal light with his own hands and fired off: "Alter your course 10 degrees to the south — I am a BATTLESHIP!"

Back came the final reply: "Alter your course 10 degrees to the north — I am a LIGHTHOUSE!"

Well, it seems that no matter how important any of us think we are, there is still a higher order. We must be subject to something more powerful than we are. That's a tough lesson for some of us to learn.

In our own little world of self-importance, there is only one thing that stands as a solid, foundational beacon for life. It's called the Word of God! You may prefer to call this book, the Bible.

By studying the Word of God, we soon discover that all other courses in life must be altered to fit this one. There is a sameness about the Word. You can read it today, or ten days from now, and it will say the same things.

Every life needs a foundation. I hope and pray that you will make God's Word your unmovable lighthouse!

Today's Quote: *It is impossible to mentally or socially enslave a Bible reading people. The principles of the Bible are the groundwork of human freedom!* — Horace Greeley

Today's Verse: Thy word have I hid in mine heart, that I might not sin against thee (Ps. 119:1:KJV).

Day 30

Authentic Empathy

A small boy wanted a puppy more than anything else. This was his dream. Every day he went to the pet shop, petted the puppies, and memorized each one's small, squirmy personality.

One afternoon he walked in and pulled $1.57 from his hip pocket. "Sir, is this enough money for a puppy?"

The answer was, "I'm sorry, Sonny, but the puppies are $25."

The lad walked back to the pen, and his hand drooped over the little wire fence around the dogs. He stroked their soft fur and spoke in quiet tones to them. The pet shop owner was touched.

"Say, young fellow, I've been thinking. Your $1.57 will do. Pick whatever puppy you like, and it's yours," said the shop owner.

The boy's eyes sparkled. He knew each dog by heart. He reached in and without hesitation pulled a certain puppy out of the pen.

The pet shop owner said, "Oh, no, you don't want that one. He's crippled. He will never run or chase balls in the park. He was born without the proper hip socket and . . . ."

The boy answered right back, "It's all right, sir." The boy lifted his pant leg, and there was a brace. He said, "I'm crippled, too. I can't run in the park either. But I need a lot of love. I'll be a good friend to this crippled puppy!"

You know, my friend, in some way we're all crippled. We all have bad days, weak moments, and flaws in our character, and we all need love!

There's a line to a song about the subject at hand: "There's just too little of — love, sweet love."

Without love, we would die. Not physically, not immediately, but something gradually happens inside to people who are forced to live without love.

The very greatest expression of love came into this world. What He did and how He came is better expressed by an unknown poet with these lines:

> I asked Jesus, "Lord, do You really love me?"
> He replied, "Yes, I really do."
> "Just how much do you love me, Lord?" I inquired
> And He said, "This much."
> Then He stretched out His hands . . . and died!

Today's Quote: *God's love for us is not a love that always exempts us from trials, but rather, a love that sees us through trials!* — Unknown

Today's Verse: How great is the love the Father has lavished on us, that we should be called children of God! And that is what we are! The reason the world does not know us is that it did not know him (1 John 3:1).